# Good Night Beautiful Mother

Written by R. Jenée Walker MD
Illustrated by Chloé Walker

# Good Night Beautiful Mother

This book is dedicated to the loving memory of my beautiful mother,

**Raphael Jean Barber**

# Hello

If you picked up this book then you or someone you care about has experienced the loss of someone you love. If you haven't you will; it is part of the circle of life. Even though I am a psychiatrist, no amount of medical school, residency, fellowship training, or review of evidence based literature eased the pain or the flood of emotion I felt as I lost my mother. Her death has been the most difficult experience of my life. After practicing medicine for many years, I know I am not alone. How do we continue to breathe without our loved one? How do we handle the aching feeling of being alone when we want to pick up the phone to call our loved one and they are not there? How do we get over feeling like an orphan even though we are grown and have our own family? Without our loved one…where did home go?

This book is not about sadness, it is about the joy and comfort we can find in remembering. It directs us toward the healing we find in the midst of our tears as we smile and remember cherished times. This book is about recognizing how remembering can foster healing and finding your joy again after a devastating loss. Familiar childhood musical jingles coming from an old time ice cream truck, catching a whiff of fresh bread baking as a breeze flows by, hearing "oldies" music from a song that "takes you way back"– these things awaken memories that bring comfort and connection.

There is something wonderful about a story. Stories connect us as one person, one race, and one family as we share emotions and feelings. The story of love, loss, and figuring out how to go on living a happy life is a story about one of the most difficult shared life experiences. There is a shared feeling and understanding that connects us all when we lose someone we treasure. When we experience loss, whether it is the loss of a mother, father, grandparent or child, a powerful, unifying awareness emerges that transcends cultures, race, age, or background and is immediately understood without a word being spoken.

"Good Night Beautiful Mother" is my story. As I share my story please know that my relationship with my mother was not perfect. She was not perfect and neither am I. Becoming a parent and experiencing the challenges of life myself have provided me with a whole new level of understanding and appreciation for my mother's own struggles and sacrifices. I know every step of the way she did her very best. Any irregular spaces or voids I have chosen to fill with gratitude. This is what I choose to focus on and remember.

At the end of the story I share **"An Epilogue: Healing Words".** Included are 14 tools I have found helpful in my own life and use daily in my practice to guide my patients toward finding their joy again. I have found these tools offer helpful insights for facing and overcoming other forms of losses including loss of relationships, jobs, health and anything that threatens our self-worth, and mental well-being. I have also included a list of resources I have found invaluable. This book is especially treasured because the artwork is drawn by my beautiful daughter Chloe as a tribute to her "Me-Me".

Grab a cup of tea, find a comfortable chair and read on. My hope is as you read "Goodnight Beautiful Mother" you will connect with your own story and remember. For you it may have been your cherished grandmother, your nurturing father, your caring aunt, teacher, mentor, or a dear friend who you leaned on and stood in the gap for you. For this reason the pictures in this book are faceless so that you can insert your own story. Imagine seeing your loved one's face, hearing their voice as you remember and relive cherished times.

Through a smile, a laugh, and perhaps a tear, my hope and prayer for you is that you find renewed peace, joy and hope as you pause…and remember.

A tender story with healing words about love that endures through life and death;

For we know that " forever love"… never dies.

## Good Night Beautiful Mother

There was once a little girl who loved her mother more than anything in the whole wide world.

As long as she could remember, her mother was the one person she could always count on.

She loved the way her mother would wake her up in the morning singing:

"Good morning to you,

Good morning to you,

I am happy to see you,

Good morning to you!"

She loved the way her mother loved her even when she would get mad and pout. One day she became so upset she decided she was going to run away from home and hid underneath the dining room table.

Her mother called her name, "frantically looking" for her as the girl watched her mother's feet from her hiding place.

She loved the warm hugs her mother gave her as she said "Oh there you are, I am so happy to see you!" as she lovingly dried the little girl's tears as she crawled from underneath the table.

She loved that every night for as long as she could remember, her mother would tuck her in bed with a warm hug and kiss and say:

"Good night beautiful daughter," and the girl would say:

"Good night beautiful mother," and the mother would say as she pulled the covers up below the girl's ears tucking her in:

"I will see you in the morning."

Good Night
beautiful
daughter...

She loved the way her mother was always kind and patient, even when she was mischievous.

On cold rainy days when the water would form deep puddles around the school, her mother would put on the girl's rain boots and button up her rain coat tight to keep her warm and dry.

As soon as her mother would drive off from school she would jump into the water and get all wet. She loved the way her mother would only gently scold as she helped her put on dry clothes so she would not get sick.

In her kindergarten Christmas program when she wore her white angel outfit, even though her halo was crooked causing her teacher to fuss, she loved the way she knew everything would be okay. The girl knew she could look out into the audience even with her tilted halo and see her mother smiling proudly back. Smiling because even though the girl couldn't keep her halo from almost falling off, her mother would believe she was the most beautiful angel ever.

She always loved the way her mother would tuck her in every night and say:

"Good night beautiful daughter," and the girl would say:

"Good night beautiful mother," and the mother would say:

"I will see you in the morning."

When she was in junior high, she loved the way her mother always encouraged her telling her she could do anything and be anything even when she felt not as smart, not as skinny, and not as pretty as everyone else.

As a teenager, she hated to shop when she had to go into the section where the clothes were labeled "chubbies". She felt so upset she cried inside. She loved the way her mother told her not to worry, that she was bright, beautiful and lovely just as she was.

She loved the way she could always look out the school window and know she would see her mother pulled up in front of the school in the old green family car that looked like a tank. Embarrassed by the car, she wished her mother would park farther down the street. Embarrassed by the car, but never by her mother whom she thought was the most beautiful mother in the whole wide world.

She loved that every evening no matter how tired her mother was, she never complained and always took time to hear about the day. When the girl shared she felt not "good enough," her mother would sing:

"You are so beautiful, so beautiful to me. You are everything I hoped for, you are everything I need, you are so very beautiful to me."

They would always then laugh together because her mother couldn't sing, but it always made the girl feel better because she knew she was loved.

She loved the Sunday dinners, the homemade pumpkin pies at Thanksgiving and all the good smells that filled the house, making it feel all warm and cozy. She loved her mother's big smile and excited "ho-ho-ho" early Christmas morning. For even though the family didn't have a lot of money the girl never realized it. Even though there were not a lot of gifts, her mother made every holiday special, and the girl truly believed she had all there was to be had.

The girl and her mother did not always agree about everything. Sometimes they had to agree to disagree, even though they both believed their opinion was right. The girl loved knowing that no matter how good or bad the day was, she was always truly loved as her mother would gently tuck her in at night and say:

"Good night beautiful daughter" and the girl would say:

"Good night beautiful mother," and the mother would say:

"I will see you in the morning."

The girl grew up and when she was in high school, she decided she wanted to become a doctor. The high school counselor called her an "overachiever" and didn't know if she could do it. Her mother encouraged her, believing she could do it and would. Because her mother believed, the girl believed and worked very hard and graduated with the highest grades in her class.

She loved the way her mother always did everything she could to help the girl fulfill her dreams.

Her mother drove three hours one way to get a book when the girl told her she thought it would help her with a difficult class for a test. Her mother never complained, always happy to do whatever she could to help.

She loved her mother for always doing without so that the girl and her brothers could have nice things. Her mother wore the same blue dress with the white stripe to church every week so that she could have dresses that were in style like the other girls.

The girl was stressed out in medical school and thought everyone was smarter, and her confidence wavered. Her mother always answered the phone no matter what time day or night, encouraging the girl in the midst of her tears and telling her she could do it and she was praying for her.

Every night when the girl was away at school, the mother called the girl and the mother would say:

"Good night beautiful daughter," and the girl would say:

"Good night beautiful mother"

And the mother would say in her kind, soothing tone,

"I will see you in the morning."

Her mother's words helped the girl to have faith in herself.

And because her mother believed she could become a doctor…the girl believed, and she worked very hard never giving up… and she became a doctor.

Time passed, and the girl got married and moved far away. Yet every night her mother would call and say:

"Good night beautiful daughter" and the girl would say:

"Good night beautiful mother."

Even though her mother was getting older and they lived far apart, the girl knew she could always count on her mother to be there for her.

No matter how old the girl was and no matter how close or how far away she was, she could count on her mother every year calling at the crack of dawn on her birthday. The girl would answer the phone met with her mother's voice singing off tune at the top of her lungs:

"Happy birthday to you,
happy birthday to you,
happy birthday beautiful daughter,
happy birthday to you."

As the years passed, the girl had children of her own, and not only did her mother love her children dearly, she always made the girl herself feel special, valued, and loved.

Days passed, years passed, and no matter where the girl was, almost every night she could count on hearing her mother's voice when she called to say "Good night beautiful daughter," and the girl would say "Good night beautiful mother."

But one day the girl's mother became ill.

The girl flew back and forth and back and forth as often as she could to see her mother. Flying back and forth because no matter how old her mother got, or how busy the girl became, she loved her mother more than anything in the whole wide world.

The girl knew that no matter where she was, or what she was doing, she could count on hearing her mother's voice saying "Good night beautiful daughter" and she would say "Good night beautiful mother." Hearing her mother's voice saying those words made the girl feel so loved.

One day the girl's brother called and said, "Sis, Mom is in the hospital and is not doing well."

The girl rushed to get on an airplane that same morning. The girl was frantic because she wanted to be there for her mother the way her mother had been there for her every day of her life.

The girl rushed off the airplane but she was too late. The girl was heartbroken. Her heart dropped below her knees. Even though the girl had tried her hardest, her mother died before she got there.

The girl was very upset, very sad and just cried. She wanted to hold her mother's hand one more time and tell her how much she loved and appreciated her every day of her life.

The girl was so shaken and so sad she became upset with God. How could He allow her mother to die without her being there to hold her hand as her beloved beautiful mother entered into her rest.

The girl did not understand. She would take walks at night and look up at the stars and wonder if her mother was the star shining brightest in the night sky.

The girl missed her mother's voice so much she would call her mother's phone number just to hear it ring even though she knew her mother was not there to answer.

The girl missed her mother so very much. She missed riding in the car holding hands singing together and laughing at the same time because they were so off key.

She missed the phone calls, especially the early morning birthday calls, and the little cards, flowers, and words of encouragement that always made her feel so very safe, special, and so very loved.

She missed the nightly phone calls and hearing her mother's sweet voice say "Good night beautiful daughter" and the girl missed saying her loving reply "Goodnight beautiful mother."

Even though the girl was grown up and had children of her own, she felt like an orphan. Because not only had she lost her mother who had been her confidant all her life, she had lost her best friend.

When the girl flew home for her high school reunion, she missed her mother who was always there to meet her at the bottom of the escalator in front of baggage claim. In her mind she saw her smiling face sitting in her wheel chair with extended arms. She drove to her mother's home and felt the vacancy and void in the house that her mother made into a home. Where did she go? Her mind knew but her heart yearned to find her. If only she could see and touch her.

At her high school reunion, the girl was excited and amazed to see so many friends from long ago. It was good they all wore nametags, because they all looked different. She was thrilled to see her friend she jumped in the puddles with in front of the grade school on rainy days. Standing next to her was her friend she sang with in the Christmas concert when wearing the angel outfit with the tilted halo. In the corner was a guy she remembered giggling over with her friends in high school but had been too shy to talk to. He was now bald and put on a few pounds.

When the girl saw her old friends they all ran to each other and squealed with joy. They laughed, shared pictures and reminisced until her classmates asked about her mother. The girl's heart sank, and her voice choked as she whispered her beautiful mother had passed away.

One by one her friends shared they too had lost someone they dearly loved. One lost her mother who at times sounded critical yet had a loving heart. Another missed her father, who was the parent she leaned on. Another classmate lost a husband, another missed a cherished grandmother and another was crushed after losing a precious child.

One by one they shared. One by one their eyes welled with tears and their voices choked. The girl now understood. She felt comfort knowing that even though each of their losses, relationships and experiences were different, they all shared the same feelings missing someone they loved more than anyone in the whole wide world.

One day she was lying in bed missing her mother tremendously and feeling very sad. The girl heard a voice within that said, "Good night beautiful daughter" and the girl found herself saying "Good night wonderful Father." And the girl knew deep within her soul that it was God's way of telling her that she was never alone.

A healing sense of peace filled her soul. In the quietness she was reminded that love never dies. She was reminded that because of God's love and His wonderful promises of heaven, we have a hope…that she and her mother will meet again.

The girl began to lift up her head and give thanks as she was reminded that a day is coming when there will be no more tears and no more sorrow and she will see her beautiful mother again…well and strong.

In that moment the girl remembered the last time she saw her mother. The girl remembered sitting by her mother's bedside and holding her mother's hand as she lovingly tucked her mother in bed pulling up the blankets gently around her shoulders and asking her if there was anything she wanted her to do.

The girl's heart became full as she remembered hearing her mother say in her quiet sweet voice with only the hum of the heater in the room whisper,

"Remember me…"

The girl knew in her heart…that she would always remember.

The girl at that moment vowed and determined that as long as she had breath…that the kindness, joy, and unselfish love that defined her mother… would live on forever in her heart.

With a new found sense of peace, confidence and hope, in the stillness and darkness the girl whispered…

"Good night beautiful mother."

In the stillness, in the quietness, the girl imagined hearing her mother's voice saying ever so sweetly…

"Good night beautiful daughter

…I will see you in the morning"

"Every new beginning comes from some other beginning's end."

– Seneca

## An Epilogue: Healing Words

## Fourteen Tools to Help You Find Your Peace and Renew Your Joy

As a psychiatrist, one thing I know for sure is that everyone experiences loss. For me, the loss of my beautiful mother crushed my soul. I once heard it said that when the soul has accomplished what it came to do, it goes. I understand that it is also said that God's time is not our time, and His ways are not always our chosen way. When you love someone, there is never an easy time to let them go. Having lost both of my parents, I understand the devastating grief of losing someone you truly love. From my own experience and hearing the shared experiences of many of my patients going through the grief process over the years, I know we are all more alike than we are different. Whether it is the loss of a mother, a father, a daughter, a son, a grandparent, an aunt, uncle, or cherished friend, the magnitude of the pain of loss is palpable. You may feel like you are going crazy and wonder if you will ever feel happy again. I would like to share with you a few words I have found helpful with the healing process. In my practice I have also found these tools useful for other forms of loss that threaten our emotional well-being such as loss of relationships, career, and self- esteem. Hang in there! In time you will feel joy again. Here are a few healing words to aid and soothe the process.

**1) Know that it is okay to cry.** There is no need to apologize or say you are sorry for crying. Crying does not mean you are weak or doing anything wrong. It simply means you miss deeply someone you love dearly. It is important to release your feelings. Internalizing your feelings can make you ill, not only physically but mentally. Some people share they have a hard time crying or they feel the need to cry and the tears do not come. Some describe feeling numb and detached. Others cry all the time. Our brains allow us to handle what we can when we are ready to handle it. Be as you are and allow yourself to feel what you feel. There is no time schedule other than your own. Know that whenever tears come, it is okay. Crying is part of the healing process.

**2) Allowing yourself to sit and experience your sadness is a vital part of the healing process but limit how much time you actively focus on your loss daily.** If you focus on loss constantly, it can consume you to the point you cannot function. In time you will be able to sit with the sadness without it totally consuming you. Be intentional about shifting your focus when your sadness begins to pull you downward. You will know when being in bed or sitting in a chair is restorative versus depleting and detrimental. When emotionally sinking, distract yourself and redirect your thoughts with loved ones, friends, work, a hobby, or acts of kindness if only for short periods of time. Allow people to love you. Feel your grief as you are able. You are on no ones' time schedule but your own. With time you will find that although your heart will continue to ache, you will be able to smile as you remember sweet memories.

**3) Anticipate difficult times such as holidays, birthdays, anniversary dates of the loss, and events such as weddings and graduations, where you know your loved one would be present if alive.** It is normal to miss them so profoundly, to feel so sad you feel as though your soul is hemorrhaging. It is lovely to in some way honor their memory on those occasions. Consider lighting a candle, place their picture in view, and mention their name. Share a fun memory, a happy time that can be re-experienced and shared by those present who loved them and are missing them as well. It is a mistake to act as though they never existed for fear of upsetting others. There is a feeling of warmth acknowledging that your loved one lived, was loved and valued. This acknowledgement keeps their memory present and your love for them alive. They will always be your mother or father. You will always be their daughter or son. This is beautiful because it acknowledges that in life and in death, they remain a vital important part of the family.

**4) Remember that love never dies.** When we say we love someone, it means we continue to love and honor them in death as well as in life. This means loving the things they stood for and the people they loved after they are gone. Their mother becomes our mother, their sisters and brothers our sisters and brothers, their children our children. As we cherish the loved ones of the deceased, our love for them lives on.

**5) Embrace the art of self-compassion.** Take time to take care of yourself. If your loved one were alive and you could hear their voice, the one thing you could do for them—that you can almost imagine hearing them say—would be to take care of yourself. Many of my patients share their loved one would be upset with them for ceasing to experience joy in their lives. Resting, exercising, eating well and being kind to ourselves is vital. By taking care of ourselves, we continue to honor the love our loved one had for us.

**6) In all ways, lead by example.** Even though our loved ones are gone, we must take care of those who remain. We still have people who love us and need us. They are still here, they count too. As parents, it is important to model for our children how to deal with whatever life brings us, the good and the bad. I often share with my patients, if you don't push forward for anyone else, do it for your children, because they are watching. You must stand so that they can stand! As we have the courage to move forward, we give our loved ones permission to move forward adding value and worth to their own lives.

**7) Know that it is okay to feel angry.** Angry at God, angry at the loved one who is gone for leaving you, angry for the way they died. Angry at how unfair it feels that others still have their mother, their child, their spouse and your beloved is gone. Angry that the lives of everyone else in the world seems to go on normally, unscathed by the magnitude of your painful loss. Angry that you want back what you once had yet you know your life is forever changed. Underlying that anger is deep seated pain. Be as you are. Scream, yell, shout, cry and let it out! I would take walks in the darkness and let those hurt feelings out. It helps you somehow feel better. These are normal, human feelings that are a painful part of the healing process. In time the anger will ease and that void will be gradually be filled with calm remembrance.

**8) Experience the freedom of forgiveness.** We all have things we wish we could have done or said differently. Sometimes we harbor feelings of anger and resentment toward the deceased if they hurt us in some way. True empowerment and freedom comes when we can forgive others as well as ourselves. We are all products of our environment and past. It is so helpful to look beyond the behavior to the reason for the behavior. It is so helpful when faced with guilt or regret to remind yourself that you did the best you could at that time with the light that you had. Holding onto hurt, anger, and regret only destroys your spirit. If someone hurt you, remind yourself that they were living with their limited light and let it go. By giving yourself the gift of forgiveness, you allow yourself to move forward toward healing and peace.

**9) Tap the healing power of humor.** There is truth to the adage that "laughter is the best medicine." Even in the midst of deepest sorrow there is healing that comes with laughter. Have you ever laughed so hard and deeply that it brought tears to your eyes? Remember thinking "That felt so good, I needed that!" In the midst of the most difficult times share a joke, watch a funny video that makes you laugh so deeply you will feel your soul smiling. Sharing a deep belly laugh with friends will not only lift your spirits but also will begin to restore your soul.

10) **Always "trust the process."** That trust means that everything that happens is part of a greater plan even when we don't understand. This trust gives us hope and a positive sense of expectancy. I truly believe that what we expect, we invite into our presence. I know that I can trust God even when I don't understand. In the midst of darkness, we find peace when we immerse in God's light and stand on His promises. It is freeing to know that faith is not based on how we feel. We have choices. We can choose hope or despair. Inner peace always follows the choice of hope.

11) **Stay in a place of gratitude.** Of course, it is unrealistic to feel thankful about the loss of a loved one. But we can be thankful that we were so blessed to have had someone in our life who we loved, no matter how long or brief the time. The love that leads to such deep feelings of loss is something that some never experience. A spirit of gratitude enables us to look around even at our darkest moments and find something to be thankful for. Darkness and light cannot occupy the same space. Be intentional about focusing on what is versus on what is not. A spirit of gratitude will lift your mood, increase your energy and lead you to greater peace as you face each day adjusting to a new normal. Remember lasting healing and inner peace begin and end with gratitude.

**12) Stand on God's Promises.** Be ever mindful that God is in control. We can look forward to that day promised in Revelation 21:4: "He will wipe every tear from their eyes. There will be no more death or sorrow or crying or pain." I am so thankful we have this hope. It is this hope that enables us to trump despair.

Remind yourself that love is eternal and defies death. Romans 8:38 says, "Nothing can ever separate us from the love of God, Neither death nor life." Vow that every day of your life, all that was of value and virtue that your loved one cherished will live forever in your life. Let their life legacy live on through you. As long as you have breath, they live! This realization keeps us motivated and pressing forward even when we don't feel it.

**13) Dare to begin to create a dream, a vision of something that gives you a feeling of hope.** Begin to believe that it is possible for you to feel happy and fulfilled again even if that feeling is fleeting and lasts only a moment. You will feel happy again. It is normal for the feelings of yearning and longing for your loved one to weave in and out of the recesses of your soul for the rest of life.

You will find in time that the yearning will not be a hindrance to hold you back but rather a powerful force to propel you forward. Eventually that inner nudge will push you toward taking baby steps that will lead you to feeling fulfilled and whole again. Baby steps lead to walking, walking leads to running, running leads to soaring. Soaring leads to rising above whatever obstacle you face. All we need to do is to hold onto hope, coupled with faith, and keep moving toward your dream. As you believe, you will become! You will begin to feel excited about new quests and will begin to feel happy again. Whatever gives you an energized new breath, even if just for a moment, move toward that. It may not be big or seem important to anyone but you. If your dream is important to you, dare to dream it! Knowing your vision is uniquely yours is all that matters, because you are worth it.

**14) Be a blessing.** Remember you are still here for a reason. Each morning as you awaken take in deep breaths, conscious that you still have this gift called life.

When we lose someone we cherish, remembering them in life and in death we are forever reminded that the difference between life and death is a single breath. In the midst of your sadness and emptiness, recognize that your life still has purpose.

Strive daily to be a blessing to someone. The greatest weapon against depression is kindness and service to others. It shifts the focus from ourselves onto others and lifts the darkness every time.

I leave you with hope and blessings as you move toward your new normal. Moment by moment, day by day, we begin again. Be kind to yourself during the process. Remember there is power in coupling feelings of loss and grief with gratitude…it is the path that leads to peace and healing.

Until that wonderful day when we shall meet again… we can experience a calming quiet peace within our souls and say with confidence in the quietness of our spirit to whomever you cherish and are missing with every other thought and breath…

… "Good night beautiful son… good night beautiful daughter"

… "Good night beautiful wife. . . good night beautiful husband"

… "Good night beautiful grandmother. . .good night beautiful grandfather"

… "Good night beautiful aunt…good night beautiful uncle"

… "Good night beautiful brother… good night beautiful sister"

… "Good night beautiful friend"

… "Good night beautiful father"

… "Good night beautiful mother" …

"I love you forever…

I will see you again... in the morning."

I found these words in a tiny frame hanging on the wall in my mother's room after she passed:

*"There is a way of living that has a certain grace and beauty. It is not a constant race for what is next, rather, an appreciation of what has come before. There is a depth, and quality of experience that is lived and felt, a recognition of what is truly meaningful. These are the feelings I would like my work to inspire. This is the quality of life that I believe in." Author unknown*

It is my hope and prayer that this book will honor the love and grace that her life exemplified every day of her life.

Good Night Beautiful Mother.

. . . I Will See You In The Morning.

# Helpful Resources

## To Guide You On Your Healing Journey

1) "On Grief and Grieving: Finding the Meaning of Grief Through the Five Stages of Loss"- Elizabeth Kubler-Ross M.D. and David Kessler.

2) "Living A Life That Matters"- Rabbi Harold S. Kushner

3) "Broken Open: How Difficult Times Can Help Us Grow"- Elizabeth Lesser'

4) Ted X Talk :"Resilience- Consider the Uses of Adversity"- Madonna Badger

5) Ted X Talk: "Living Beyond Limits" – Amy Purdy

6) "Healing After Loss"- Martha Whitman Hickman

7) "Streams In The Desert" L.B.Cowan: Uplifting words to daily immerse you in light during dark times.

R. Jenée Walker MD is a psychiatrist board certified in adult, child, and adolescent psychiatry. She has a story published in Chicken Soup for the African American Women's Soul. Born and reared in Compton, California, she resides and practices in Charleston, West Virginia. She is married and is the mother of three adult children who she cherishes as her greatest blessing.

Chloé J. Walker is a medical student at Loma Linda University School of Medicine. She painted these pictures for her "Me-Me" to honor her life. She takes "joy breaks" to paint which she loves to ease the stress of medical school. She hopes to become a physician one day who uplifts and encourages the lives of others.

The light in me…

honors the brave beautiful light in you.

Remain encouraged!

This is not...

# *The End*

...but the Beginning...

# Acknowledgements

This book truly was a family effort. Special thanks to my beautiful daughter Chloé for the joy that shines through in her lovely artwork. Heartfelt thanks to my husband Bob and my sons Robbie and Jared for their help and guidance doing their computer magic. Thank you to Bonny Starkey for her expertise in directing our layout design.

With gratitude and appreciation for the many patients who have shared their hearts and souls with me over the years. It is through their grace and courage that I have gained greater humble understanding and learned valuable life lessons that have made this book possible.

Continue the healing journey with us at drrjeneewalker.com.

Made in the USA
San Bernardino, CA
17 May 2018